W9-CUJ-555

The Missions of California

Mission
San Miguel Arcángel

Kathleen J. Edgar and Nancy A. Edgar

The Rosen Publishing Group's
PowerKids Press™
New York

Published in 2000, 2003 by The Rosen Publishing Group, Inc.
29 East 21st Street, New York, NY 10010

Copyright © 2000, 2003 by The Rosen Publishing Group, Inc.

All rights reserved. No part of this book may be reproduced in any form without permission in writing from the publisher, except by a reviewer.

Photo Credits and Photo Illustrations: pp. 1, 17, 18, 21, 27, 35, 36, 42, 43, 44, 45, 48, 50, 51, 52, 57 by Cristina Taccone; pp. 4, 20, 26, 32, 39 © Shirley Jordan; p. 6 © The Bridgeman Art Library International Ltd.; pp. 8, 12 © Seaver Center for Western History Research, LA County Museum of Natural History; p. 9 © AP/Wide World; pp. 11, 14, by Tim Hall; pp. 33, 34, 36, 37, 40, 41 © Michael K. Ward; p. 19 © Eda Rogers; p. 22, 49 © SuperStock; pp. 24, 31, 38 © Santa Barbara Mission Archive—Library; p. 46 © The Huntington Library, Art Collections, and Botanical Gardens, San Marino, California/SuperStock; p. 47 © Stock Montage.

Revised Edition 2003

Book Design: Danielle Primiceri

Book Layout: Felicity Erwin

Editorial Consultant Coordinator: Karen Fontanetta, M.A., Curator, Mission San Miguel Arcángel
Editorial Consultant: Karen Fontanetta, M.A.
Historical Photo Consultants: Thomas L. Davis, M.Div., M.A. and Michael K. Ward, M.A.

Edgar, Kathleen J.
    Mission San Miguel Arcángel / by Kathleen J. Edgar and Nancy A. Edgar
      p. cm. — (The missions of California)
    Includes bibliographical references and index.
    Summary: Discusses Mission San Miguel Arcángel from its founding in 1797 to the present day, including the reasons for Spanish colonization in California and the effects of colonization on the California Indians.
    ISBN 0-8239-5896-5 (lib. bdg.)
    1. Mission San Miguel Arcángel (San Miguel, Calif.)—History Juvenile literature.
    2. Spanish mission buildings—California—San Miguel Region—History Juvenile literature.
    3. Franciscans—California—San Miguel Region—History Juvenile literature. 4. Indians of North America—Missions—California—San Miguel Region—History Juvenile literature. 5. California—History—To 1846 Juvenile literature. [1. Mission San Miguel Arcángel (San Miguel, Calif.)—History. 2. Missions—California. 3. Indians of North America—Missions—California. 4. California—History—To 1846.] I. Edgar, Nancy A. II. Title. III. Series.
    F869. M666E34 1999
    979.4'78—dc21
                                                     99-20507
                                                  CIP

Manufactured in the United States of America

Contents

Spanish Explorers Come to California

Mission San Miguel Arcángel

On the outskirts of a sleepy little California town the past is preserved at Mission San Miguel Arcángel. As cars race on highways around the town of San Miguel, the quiet mission stands as a reminder of Spanish efforts to colonize the land that is today the state of California. At one end of the mission stands the church, an off-white building with a red tile roof. Next to the church is a short wall with several entrances.

Mission San Miguel Arcángel was founded by Spanish friars and soldiers in 1797 and built by the Salinan Indians. The friars, called *frays* in Spanish, were religious men who devoted their lives to the Catholic religion. They were sent by the Spanish government to colonize lands in the Americas. The friars established a chain of missions along the coast. They hoped to convert California Indians to Catholicism and teach them the Spanish way of life. Mission San Miguel Arcángel was the 16th of 21 missions founded in California between 1769 and 1823.

Spain Explores the Americas

Spain's interest in California began in 1493, after explorer Christopher Columbus brought back news of the lands he called the New World, or North America, South America, and Central America. Although American Indians had lived on these lands for thousands of years, the Americas were unknown to European settlers until this time. The Spanish and other Europeans were eager to explore these lands and claim them for themselves.

◀ *This is the church of Mission San Miguel Arcángel.*

The Spanish were interested in the New World for a number of reasons. They wanted to make their empire larger so they could become a more powerful nation. They hoped to find gold, spices, and other riches. They also wanted to spread the teachings of Christianity.

New Spain

The king of Spain wanted to claim land in the Americas, but Spain didn't have many citizens who wanted to settle there. In order to take command of these lands without sending a large number of settlers, the Spanish government decided to turn the American Indians into Spanish citizens. They would do this by teaching the American Indians the Spanish language, customs, and religious beliefs. In 1519, a Spanish soldier and explorer named Hernán Cortés went to the area that today is Mexico and began conquering the great Aztec empire. The Spanish claimed this land and called it New Spain. They established a capital that they named Mexico City and set up a government under a leader called a viceroy. The king sent Spanish soldiers and friars to build religious settlements, or missions, that would teach the conquered people in New Spain about the Spanish religion and way of life.

This picture, painted around 1550, shows Cortés entering the Aztec lands.

Alta California

After the Spanish claimed New Spain, they became interested in some of the land to the north. This land is now California and the part of Mexico that is called the Baja Peninsula. The state of California was then called Alta, or upper, California, while the Baja Peninsula was known as Baja, or lower, California.

The Spanish explorer Juan Rodríguez Cabrillo sailed to Alta California in 1542, where he found what was later called San Diego Bay. Cabrillo and his men claimed the land for Spain by planting a cross in the ground to represent their country and its religion.

In 1602, another Spanish explorer, Sebastían Vizcaíno, traveled to Alta California.

The missions labeled in dark print were founded before Mission San Miguel Arcángel. The lighter print shows the missions founded later. ▶

San Francisco Solano
San Rafael Arcángel
San Francisco de Asís
San José
Santa Clara de Asís
Santa Cruz
San Juan Bautista
San Carlos Borromeo de Carmelo
Nuestra Señora de la Soledad
San Antonio de Padua
San Miguel Arcángel
San Luis Obispo de Tolosa
La Purísima Concepción
Santa Inés
Santa Bárbara
San Buenaventura
San Fernando Rey de España
San Gabriel Arcángel
San Juan Capistrano
San Luis Rey de Francia
San Diego de Alcalá

He sailed around what is now the Bay of Monterey. Since neither Cabrillo nor Vizcaíno found gold or rich nations to conquer, the Spanish did not think it was worth the time and money necessary to colonize Alta California.

It wasn't until 1769 that the Spanish sent soldiers and friars to begin the Alta California missions. At that time, Russian settlers were moving down toward Alta California from Alaska. The Spanish king, Carlos III, feared that colonists from Russia and Britain would take over these lands. King Carlos III ordered the government in New Spain to establish two missions in Alta California as fast as possible. One of the missions was to be built in San Diego and the other was to be built in Monterey, about 450 miles (724 km) to the north.

▲
Captain Gaspár de Portolá

The Spanish Settle Alta California

The government in New Spain sent five groups to Alta California under the military command of Captain Gaspár de Portolá. A Franciscan friar named Fray Junípero Serra was chosen as the president of the mission system in Alta California. He accompanied one of these groups. Serra had devoted his life to missionary work in New Spain and went to Alta California when he was 55 years old.

The expedition included soldiers, friars, and Indians who had converted to Christianity at missions in New Spain. Three ships, the *San Carlos*, the *San Antonio*, and the *San José*, sailed up the coast. Two groups traveled over the desert land of New Spain.

8

All five groups were to meet near San Diego Bay at the beginning of July. The journey was difficult, and many men became sick. The *San José* and its crew were lost at sea. More than half of the 219 sailors who started the journey to Alta California died.

The Spanish ships carried many materials the friars would need to begin the missions, including food supplies and religious articles like crosses, statues, and robes. Other supplies were loaded on the backs of the pack mules that made the overland journey. Those who traveled over land herded cattle to Alta California from missions in New Spain.

The groups met in San Diego, and on July 16, 1769, Fray Serra founded Mission San Diego de Alcalá, the first mission in Alta California. It would be almost another 30 years before the Spanish would begin to build Mission San Miguel Arcángel.

When the first mission was founded in Alta California in 1769, many American Indians already lived there in small villages. In contrast the eastern coast of North America had many large cities, such as Boston, New York, and Philadelphia. Members of 13 eastern colonies signed the Declaration of Independence seven years later, in 1776.

The Salinan Indians

The Salinan

Before the Spanish colonized Alta California, about 300,000 California Indians lived there. There were many different groups of Native Americans and each group spoke its own language. The California Indians of the San Miguel area mainly belonged to the Salinan tribe, although some may have been Chumash Indians.

The Salinan lived like many other groups of California Indians. Although the Salinan did not have a written history, people who study past civilizations, called archaeologists, have learned about them by carefully digging up sites where their villages used to be. They have uncovered artifacts, such as tools and weapons, that show how the Salinan Indians lived many years ago.

Hunting and Gathering

The lifestyle of the Salinan was based on the natural world. Their homes, diet, work, and religion were all linked to nature. The Salinan ate food they could collect, hunt, or catch. Much of the Salinan's daily life was spent looking for plants, animals, fish, and insects. Salinan women did most of the gathering. They collected roots, seeds, berries, and nuts, including acorns. They also searched for insects and worms.

Acorns were an important source of nutrition for the Salinan, as they were for many California Indians. Acorns were used in soups, cakes, and breads. The Salinan collected acorns in the fall and stored them for later use. However, acorns have a bitter acid that makes them taste very bad. To make the acorns taste better, the Salinan women

The Salinan Indians fished with spears or nets. ▶

▲

Salinan women wore skirts made of tule grass like this one.

prepared them in a special way. First they ground the acorns by crushing them between two rocks, called a mortar and pestle. They placed the acorn flour in a sandy pit or a basket and poured hot water over it. This had to be done 10 times to make the acorn flour ready to eat.

The Salinan men fished with nets woven from grass. They hunted with spears and bows and arrows, for deer, ducks, rabbits, squirrels, and birds. Their arrowheads and spear tips were made of rocks chipped to form a hard point that could pierce an animal's skin. The Salinan men used strong, flexible tree branches to make their bows. They made bow strings from vegetable stalks or animal tendons, called sinews.

Homes

The Salinan built their homes in the shape of a cone, using materials that grew in the area. They used wood to make a cone-shaped frame, then tied layers of brush and tule grass thatching to it. The thatch worked like shingles to keep the rain out.

The Salinan lived in villages of 30 to 300 people. They moved their villages at different times during the year. Since they lived off the land, they had to move when water or food in the area became scarce. They also moved when their homes became old, weathered, or unstable.

In the fall, the Salinan moved to temporary shelters near forests of oak trees so they could harvest as many acorns as possible.

Dress

Throughout much of the year, the Salinan men wore little or no clothing. The women wore skirts made out of bark, grass, or animal hides. In cooler weather, men and women draped hides over their shoulders for warmth. The Salinan wore necklaces and earrings made of abalone shells. Both men and women wore their hair long.

Religion

The Salinan believed many spirits were at work in nature. They believed that medicine men, or shamans, were able to cure illnesses by chasing away evil spirits. The shamans treated the sick by dancing, singing, and using herbal medicines.

The Salinan honored the spirits with ceremonies. They also performed rituals to acknowledge deaths, weddings, hunting trips, births, and when boys and girls entered into adulthood. These ceremonies included singing and dancing. Sometimes the Salinan painted their bodies or wore special costumes for these occasions.

The Salinan had a lot of personal freedom. They set their own work schedule and found time to enjoy games, singing, and dancing. They were free to travel on hunting trips, to trade with other tribes, and to visit other villages. When the Spanish came to Alta California, the Salinan's way of life changed forever.

The Mission System

Friars and Soldiers

Before the Spanish came to Alta California, they had already founded many missions in New Spain and Baja California. They knew that the best way to draw California Indians to the missions was to provide them with food and gifts. After the Indians began to live at the missions, they would be taught the Spanish language, customs, and religion.

Although the Spanish government wanted to build missions to create more Spanish citizens and claim land for Spain, the friars went to the missions because they were eager to teach California Indians about Christianity. They believed that only Christians would go to heaven after they died, and they wanted to save the American Indians' souls.

Soldiers were sent to help with the building of the mission complex, to watch over the Indians at the mission, and to protect the complex against local California Indians who didn't want the Spanish on their lands. Each mission had four or five soldiers who lived in the complex. In some areas, the Spanish built forts called presidios to protect the missions from attack.

The Spanish and the Salinan

The Salinan lived very differently than the Europeans did. The Spanish regarded the Salinan as people who were "uncivilized," or as children who needed to be taught to live "properly." These prejudices were based on many things, including the fact that the Salinan wore little or no clothing, while the Spanish men wore shirts,

The friars thought that they were helping the California Indians by bringing them to the missions.

jackets, and trousers, and the Spanish women wore floor-length dresses. The Spanish saw the Salinan Indians as inferior because the Indians were not educated in schools, they lived in temporary homes, and they worshiped many spirits instead of the Christian god. The Spanish wanted to help the Salinan by teaching them how to farm, speak the Spanish language, and follow the Christian religion. The Spanish thought that teaching the Indians how to live like Spaniards was in the best interest of the Indians. They didn't realize that the Salinan led productive lives on their own.

When California Indians joined a mission and converted to Christianity, they were called neophytes, which meant that they were new to the faith. Neophytes had to live at the mission and were not allowed to leave without the friars' permission. The friars feared that if the neophytes left the mission, they might never return.

The Spanish hoped to train the neophytes in the Spanish way of life in 10 years. After this period of time, the Spanish planned to turn the mission lands over to the Indians. The Indians would operate the mission as Spanish citizens and pay taxes to the Spanish government. The land would remain under the control of New Spain. This process of taking control of the land away from religious leaders and giving it to the government is called secularization.

While the original plan may have been to take over California Indian lands only to return them later, this did not happen. European, Mexican, and American settlers would keep most of the lands that once belonged to California Indian tribes.

The friars believed that by educating the children ▶
it would be easier to convert the adults. ▶

The Founding of Mission San Miguel Arcángel

Fray Lasuén

Mission San Miguel Arcángel was founded 28 years after Fray Serra founded the first mission in Alta California. Fray Serra died in 1784, and Fray Fermín Francisco de Lasuén became the new mission president on February 6, 1785. As president of the missions in Alta California, Lasuén made sure that each mission had everything it needed. He was also in charge of founding new missions. Fray Lasuén founded Mission San Miguel Arcángel.

✝ FRANCISCAN MISSION
SAN MIGUEL
FOUNDED 1797
✝

▲ *This sign commemorates the mission's founding.*

Choosing a Site

In 1795, the governor of California, Governor Diego Borica, decided that there was too large a gap between Mission San Luis Obispo de Tolosa and Mission San Antonio de Padua. It was more than a day's journey, and the Spanish did not like to travel at night through Indian lands. Governor Borica sent an expedition to find a suitable site for a new mission between the two that were already there. Fray Buenaventura Sitjar of Mission San Antonio de Padua and a few soldiers formed this expedition. Fray Sitjar wrote to Fray Lasuén that he had found a good spot with the necessary sources of water and timber nearby.

Governor Borica wrote to the viceroy of New Spain, Viceroy Branciforte, to ask for permission to build the mission and for 1,000

This is a statue of Fray Lasuén, the second president of the California Missions. ▶

The major source of water for Mission San Miguel was the nearby Salinas River.

pesos for supplies. On August 19, 1796, Viceroy Branciforte wrote to say that the building could begin.

The site that Fray Sitjar chose for Mission San Miguel Arcángel was near the Salinas River. Located in a fertile valley with rich soil, the land was ideal for farming and ranching. The site was also near a large Salinan village called Cholam. The Spanish hoped that many Salinan from this village would join the mission.

On July 25, 1797, Fray Lasuén founded Mission San Miguel Arcángel. Accompanied by Fray Sitjar and a few soldiers, Fray Lasuén blessed the spot, raised a cross, and performed a Christian church service called Mass. Fray Sitjar and a friar named Fray Antonio de la Concepción Horra were the first missionaries at Mission San Miguel Arcángel.

Salinan Come to the Mission

Many of the Salinan who came to the founding had friends and relatives who lived at Mission San Antonio de Padua and at Mission San Luis Obispo de Tolosa. They were interested in learning more about the Spanish way of life, but mostly, they were attracted by the steady supply of food that the mission could provide.

After the founding ceremony, the friars baptized 15 Salinan children. Baptism is a ritual that is held when someone is accepted into the Christian religion. The friars were pleased that the Salinan wanted to join Mission San Miguel Arcángel.

The Spanish needed the Salinan's help to build the mission complex. Some of the Salinan wanted to try the Spanish tools. The Spanish used axes made of metal, which could chop down trees quickly. The Indians used stone and wood tools, which didn't cut wood as easily. Other Salinan were attracted to the mission by gifts of food, beads, and fabrics offered by the Spanish in return for their work. Building began right away.

Mission San Miguel Arcángel is named after Saint Michael the Archangel. In paintings and statues, Saint Michael is often shown with his sword raised. He is said to guard people from the devil.

21

Building Mission San Miguel Arcángel

Temporary Shelters and Early Buildings

After the founding ceremony, Fray Lasuén left the mission. Fray Sitjar was in charge, and Fray Horra assisted him. The friars, soldiers, and the Salinan at the mission built temporary shelters out of wooden planks and thatch, designed to last only until more permanent structures could be built.

After the shelters were built, the friars, soldiers, and neophytes began to make adobe bricks for more permanent buildings. The Spanish showed the Salinan how to mix mud, water, and straw to make adobe. The workers mixed the adobe with their feet and packed it into rectangular wooden molds. Once the bricks were molded, the workers placed them in the sun to dry. Mud was used to cement the bricks together to make walls. After the walls were completed, a roof was built of sticks and mud.

Fray Horra

Fray Sitjar, Fray Horra, and the neophytes at Mission San Miguel Arcángel worked hard. They had few supplies, and there was much to be done. Fray Horra had trouble adjusting to mission life. Soon after he arrived at Mission San Miguel Arcángel, Fray Horra wrote to the viceroy of New Spain that the Franciscans in California were mistreating the neophytes. He said that the friars beat and shackled the Indians at the missions. Fray Horra did not like the way the neophytes were treated, and he did not like being at Mission San Miguel Arcángel. The work was difficult, and he was far from his home, family, and culture. The stress of life at the mission was too much for Fray Horra.

◀ *The neophytes worked hard to make enough adobe bricks to build the mission.*

23

Before a month had passed, Horra became mentally unstable. He ranted, shouted, and shot at some of the Salinan. The Spanish sent him back to New Spain.

Two New Friars

Fray Horra was replaced by Fray Juan Francisco Martín, who joined the mission on December 3, 1797. He was a talented builder and helped the neophytes with their work. He took the time to learn the Salinan language so that he could communicate with the neophytes at the mission.

After Fray Martín's arrival, work at Mission San Miguel Arcángel continued, and by the end of the month, three buildings were finished. One was a large building, 71 feet (21.6 m) by 17 feet (5.2 m), made of boards. There was also an adobe house, which

Cattle were very important at the mission. They provided milk, meat, and leather.

measured 57 feet (17.4 m) by 17 feet (5.2 m). A small adobe chapel, 28 feet (8.5 m) by 34 feet (10.4 m), was also built. All three of these buildings had roofs made of sticks and mud, which were then covered with grass.

At this time, the mission had 130 cows and bulls and 531 sheep. Most of these animals had been donated by nearby missions so that ranching could begin at Mission San Miguel Arcángel. Farming had begun also, and wheat, corn, barley, and beans were planted and harvested.

In August 1799, Fray Sitjar left Mission San Miguel Arcángel to return to Mission San Antonio de Padua. Fray Baltasar Carnicier came to Mission San Miguel Arcángel to assist Fray Martín. By December 31, 1800, five more adobe buildings with mud roofs had been built. These included a dormitory, called a *monjerío*, for unmarried neophyte women and girls, a granary for storing grain, and a permanent adobe dwelling for the friars, called a *convento*.

A Poisoning

Everything seemed to be going well at Mission San Miguel Arcángel until 1801, when Fray Martín and Fray Carnicier got sick. They developed severe stomach pains and thought that some of the neophytes might have poisoned them. Fray Francisco Pujol came down from Mission San Antonio de Padua to help the two friars, and he became sick as well. Fray Martín and Fray Carnicier got better, but Fray Pujol died after returning to his own mission. The friars accused some of the neophytes of poisoning them and had the neophytes beaten for the crime. Later, people realized that the neophytes probably had been wrongfully accused. Fray Lasuén wrote in his journals that the true cause of the poisonings was a copper container lined with tin that held the friars' liquor. He believed that the container had become toxic, poisoning the drink. Today, some scholars believe that the friars were already sick and that the neophytes tried to heal them by giving them herbal medicines. The friars may not have been used to these herbal medicines, and the herbs could have made them sicker.

The Building Continues

By 1804, hundreds of Salinan had converted to Christianity and come to live at the mission. Mission San Miguel Arcángel had all the spinning wheels, looms, and wool it needed for the women to begin weaving blankets and cloth and making clothes. This became one of the principal industries at the mission. The neophytes were successfully raising oxen, cattle, horses, sheep, mules, and pigs. Crops were planted and harvested in greater quantities than ever before.

The year 1805 was an important year for building. The neophytes constructed 47 houses for the neophyte village, called a *ranchería*, just outside the mission. Mission San Miguel Arcángel had made great progress in just a few years.

▲

Looms such as this were used to make material and blankets. The wool came from the mission sheep.

A Fire and Its Effects

On August 25, 1806, a devastating fire swept through Mission San Miguel Arcángel. The blaze destroyed two rows of buildings, the church roof, and more than 6,000 bushels of grain. The friars and the neophytes were discouraged but determined to continue their work. Nearby missions sent food and other materials to help the residents rebuild the damaged buildings.

Restoration began soon after the fire. Many of the buildings were only in need of repairs. Some of the weaving rooms and workshops had to be entirely rebuilt. At the same time, 27 new homes for the neophytes were constructed in the *ranchería*.

One of the reasons that the fire had spread so quickly was because the roofs were made of mud, sticks, and thatch. These materials caught fire easily. The friars decided to build tile roofs instead. They showed the neophytes how to make tiles from water and clay. The tiles were rounded by molding the wet clay mixture against logs. Then they were left to dry in the sun. The

Tools like these, which were used to build the mission, had to be shipped to California from Mexico and Spain.

tiles would be much more fire resistant than the roofs that contained sticks and thatch.

Although Mission San Miguel Arcángel had suffered a setback, the Salinan continued to live and work there. At the end of 1806, there were 949 neophytes at the mission and its *ranchería*.

The Finishing Touches

When making the walls, the workers had left holes in the buildings for windows. Glass was difficult to get in Alta California. Instead of covering the windows with glass, neophytes greased and stretched sheepskin over the openings to keep out the cold, rain, and flies. The skin wasn't clear like glass, but it allowed some light to enter the buildings.

Once the tile roofs were finished, the neophytes plastered the walls. To make the plaster, they mixed sand, water, cactus juice, and lime. Lime is a powder made from calcium in rocks or seashells. The neophytes smoothed the plaster over the rough adobe bricks.

As more buildings were added to the mission, they were placed in the shape of a quadrangle, or hollow square. In the center of the mission quadrangle was a courtyard. As the construction continued, the complex was expanded so that it eventually included the *convento*, *monjerío*, *ranchería*, dining rooms, kitchens, study rooms, workshops, granaries, stables, a corral, and a cemetery.

Ranchos

The lands surrounding the mission were used for planting crops and raising livestock. The mission grew so large that the friars established several *ranchos* for raising livestock. The *ranchos* usually had a chapel, stables, a corral, and housing for the neophytes. These were built miles (km) from the main mission complex so the friars could work with the

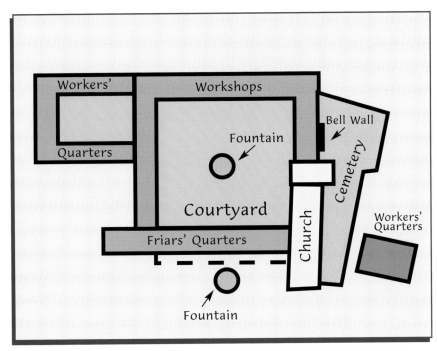

Workers' Quarters, Workshops, Bell Wall, Fountain, Cemetery, Courtyard, Church, Workers' Quarters, Friars' Quarters, Fountain

▲

This is a diagram of Mission San Miguel Arcángel. The quadrangle was the center of mission life. The ranchos were further away, in the surrounding countryside.

American Indians who lived in these areas. The *ranchos* at Mission San Miguel Arcángel included Rancho la Playa at San Simeón, Rancho de la Asunción, Rancho del Aguaje, Rancho el Paso de Robles, Rancho Santa Rosa, and Rancho Santa Ysabel.

The first *rancho* was begun in 1810, when a house and granary were built at Rancho la Playa. The rest of the *ranchos* were built between 1810 and 1820. There were hot springs at Rancho el Paso de Robles and Rancho de la Asunción that the friars and neophytes used during the cold, damp winters. The *ranchos* greatly added to Mission San Miguel Arcángel's ability to attract more neophytes and to farm and raise livestock.

Life at Mission San Miguel Arcángel

Change for the Salinan

When the Salinan came to join Mission San Miguel Arcángel, their way of life greatly changed. The neophytes were treated as children and had to obey the friars. They could not make their own decisions about what they wanted to do or wear. They could not worship the spirits of the Salinan religion. In addition to this lack of basic freedom, the neophytes had to follow a daily routine of work and prayer. The missionaries were used to living lives that followed a strict schedule. The Salinan were not. Many neophytes had trouble adapting to the highly structured lifestyle of the friars, but some felt it was worth it.

The Daily Routine

The mission bells woke the neophytes at dawn. They gathered for church services, followed by Bible lessons. The women then served a breakfast of *atole*, a mush made of grain or corn. Next, the friars gave everyone his or her work assignment. The men labored in the fields, orchards, *ranchos*, and workshops, while the women tended the children and made food, baskets, cloth, and soap.

The Salinan men grew corn, peas, beans, and barley. They also learned how to make charcoal, which was used for fuel and in paints. On the *ranchos*, they tended to the livestock, which included sheep, cattle, horses, mules, oxen, pigs, and goats. The Salinan men also worked in the mission's workshops to perfect skills in blacksmithing, carpentry, tanning, and making tiles and adobe. When the mission needed repairs, the men worked with the friars to rebuild or refinish the buildings.

Bells were used to call the neophytes to Mass. This bell was built in 1897. The picture shows ▶ a friar ringing the bell in the 1930s.

Chairs like these had seats that were made from hides.

The Salinan women made food for the residents at the mission. They learned Spanish cooking techniques and began to use corn and wheat flour instead of acorn flour. Women were taught to spin yarn out of the wool from sheep raised at the mission. They were taught to weave on looms so they could make blankets and European-style clothing. They made soap by using fat from animals, called tallow, and ashes.

After the morning work session, the women served a lunch of *pozole*, a soup made of grain with a little meat and vegetables. Then it was time for a *siesta*, or rest. Work continued in the afternoon, followed by Mass, supper, and prayers. In the evening, the neophyte boys were taught Spanish and religious lessons. Then everyone had time to relax. The Salinan liked to play games, sing, and dance.

Holidays

Everyone at Mission San Miguel Arcángel celebrated church holidays or other occasions with festivals, called *fiestas*. The Spanish holidays were often in honor of Jesus or Catholic saints. The Salinan liked to perform their traditional ceremonies, even though they were not part of their new Catholic faith. While the friars did not approve of these rituals, they often allowed them. They believed it was more important to keep the neophytes happy. They didn't want the Salinan to get upset and try to leave the mission.

▲
The Indians sometimes performed their own traditional ceremonies even though the friars discouraged it.

Mission San Miguel Arcángel Continues to Grow

A New Church

By 1814, there were around 2,000 neophytes at Mission San Miguel Arcángel. This was the greatest number of neophytes that would ever live there. Fray Martín and Fray Cabot, who had come to replace Fray Carnicier, decided that there were so many neophytes at Mission San Miguel Arcángel that a new church was needed. They wrote to ask the governor of California, Governor José Argüello, for a permit to build a larger church.

While the friars were waiting for the governor's response, Fray Cabot decided to set out on an expedition to bring more California Indians to the mission. On October 2, 1814, Fray Cabot and a soldier traveled east to a Yokut Indian village called Bubal. That day Fray Cabot baptized 22 Yokuts. Twenty of these were over 80 years old. Two others were in their 30s, but were very ill and about to die. It was much easier for the friars to get sick or old people to agree to be baptized than to get healthy adults to convert. The friars believed that only Christians who had been baptized would go to heaven. They told sick or dying people about the terrible things

Mission San Miguel never had a bell wall or tower until a modern one was built in the 1950s.

◄ The friars baptized adults only after a period of education and understanding of what it meant to be Christian.

The neophytes made thousands of adobe bricks for the new church.

that might happen to them if they didn't go to heaven after they died. When California Indians who were dying heard this, they often agreed to convert.

Fray Cabot left the village of Bubal the next day and traveled to another Yokut village called Sumtache. The Yokuts thought that the Spaniards had come to attack them, and a fight broke out. Two Yokut women and two horses were killed. Fray Cabot returned home to Mission San Miguel Arcángel.

On December 14, 1814, Governor Argüello gave Fray Martín and Fray Cabot permission

Each adobe brick weighs about 50 pounds (19 kg).

to build the first permanent church at the mission. The friars spent over a year planning and gathering the necessary materials. The neophytes made and stored adobe bricks. In 1816, the stone foundation for the new church was laid. Work continued steadily over the next two years, and in 1819, the new church was finished.

An Attack on the Mission

In 1818, Yokuts from the San Joaquin Valley confronted the Spanish in two battles away from the main complex. The Yokuts may have been angry that the missionaries were taking more and more land in Alta California. The Yokuts who attacked the soldiers found that their bows and arrows were no match for the guns of the Spanish soldiers. They were forced to give up the fight when the soldiers shot back at them with bullets.

The Yokuts and the Spanish fought two battles near Mission San Miguel Arcángel in 1818.

Hardships of Mission Life

Hardships for the Spanish

Life at Mission San Miguel Arcángel presented challenges for everyone living there. The buildings had dirt floors, the blankets were coarse and scratchy, and the food was often bland. The missionaries and soldiers were far away from their homes and families, and they often felt isolated. The friars had to manage large farms and try to keep hundreds of neophytes happy with their life at the mission.

The friars slept on beds with no mattresses and only one blanket.

Hardships for the Neophytes

Many of the Salinan at Mission San Miguel Arcángel did not like their loss of freedom. Some neophytes had come to the mission only for the food and shelter it provided. They did not like being forced to obey the friars and being punished if they failed to obey. Some neophytes were unhappy with mission life and wanted to leave. To ease the tension at the mission, the friars allowed the Indians to choose *alcaldes*, who were like police officers. They communicated between the friars and the neophytes and tried to keep things peaceful. They also helped to oversee the neophytes' work, and they punished those who were lazy or did not do their jobs well.

Life at Mission San Miguel Arcángel was often difficult for both the Spanish and the Salinan.

Some neophytes tried to escape. The friars sent soldiers and *alcaldes* to bring them back. Runaways were beaten. This discouraged others from trying to leave. Another common punishment was locking neophytes in the stocks. Stocks were wooden frames that had holes to hold a prisoner's wrists or

Neophytes were sometimes punished by the Spanish soldiers. Both Spaniards and Indians were punished with whippings when they broke the rules.

ankles to keep him or her confined. At various missions throughout Alta California, the punishments could be very brutal. Word of this treatment spread throughout the mission system and territory, causing fear and anger among some of the Indians.

Illness

Sickness was common at Mission San Miguel Arcángel and caused many deaths. The neophytes were exposed to European diseases for the first time. These diseases included chicken pox, syphilis, measles, and smallpox. While some of these illnesses didn't kill Europeans, they were very harmful to the California Indians, whose bodies had not developed any resistance to them. As a result, many died.

Living quarters were often crowded and sometimes unsanitary. The Salinan women got sick from being inside the *monjerío* for much of the day and all through the night. Since the buildings were constructed with adobe, the air was damp and cool inside. This caused breathing problems for some people.

The mission system had its advantages and its drawbacks. While it offered the benefits of food and shelter, it also contributed to disease, death, and the loss of freedom for the Salinan.

▲
Many Salinan died because they were not immune to European diseases brought to the New World by the Spanish.

The Decline of Mission San Miguel Arcángel

New Spain Becomes Mexico

In 1821, Mexico gained its independence from Spain after an 11-year war. Alta California and the mission chain became the property of the Mexican government. Ten years later, the Mexican government decided to take control of the mission lands away from the church, an act called secularization. The Spanish had originally planned to secularize all the missions after 10 years, but this had not happened. The friars didn't want the missions to be secularized because they didn't believe that the Indians could operate the missions on their own.

Decoration of the Church

During this period, fewer Salinan were joining Mission San Miguel Arcángel, so new buildings did not need to be built. Fray Cabot asked a friend named Estévan Munras to come help the neophytes paint pictures on the walls inside the church. Munras helped design the bright and colorful frescoes inside the mission church.

The artists at Mission San Miguel Arcángel had to make their own paints. To do this, they added linseed oil or cactus juice to dyes and pigments. Most dyes were made from materials that could be found in the area. Yellow was created with a clay called ochre. Mercury ore made red, and copper ore made green. Black came from charcoal.

▲
Pigments made from soil, flowers, and berries were used to make paint.

Mission San Miguel Arcángel's altar wall is covered with religious symbols and designs. This is the only ▶ mission which still has all of the original paintings on its walls.

▲
Statue of Saint Anthony, holding the Christ Child

Munras wanted to paint designs that would make the inside of the church of Mission San Miguel Arcángel look like ancient Roman buildings. Since the mission didn't have the materials to build detailed doorways, arches, balconies, and pillars, Munras and the neophytes painted them instead. The artists used a technique called marbleizing, which made objects look like they were carved from marble. These paintings created the illusion that the arches and pillars were actually there.

In front of the church sanctuary is an altar. Behind the altar is the reredos, a large backboard, that has an eye painted on it. This represents the all-seeing eye of God. Below are three statues. A statue of the mission's namesake, Saint Michael, is in the center. Statues of Saint Anthony, the patron saint of the poor, and Saint Francis of Assisi, the founder of the Franciscan order, are on either side. The friars used these objects when teaching the neophytes religious lessons. They used the statues and pictures to illustrate their stories.

▲
Statue of Saint Francis of Assisi, founder of the Franciscan order

Secularization

Fray Martín died at the mission in 1824. Fray Cabot took charge of Mission San Miguel Arcángel. Soon after, major changes began to take place. In 1834, the Mexican government passed laws to secularize the missions. This meant that the neophytes would be free citizens of Spain.

Although the government said that the neophytes were free from the rule of the friars, it made it legal for the Mexican officials to force the California Indians to work the land that was taken from the Catholic Church. On January 6, 1831, the Mexican governor of California, Governor Echeandia issued a decree saying that the missions would be secularized. That day, four Mexican officials came to Mission San Miguel Arcángel to free the neophytes from the friars. One of the officials, José Castro, assembled the Salinan at the mission and told them that they were free to leave. The Salinan asked if they could consider the offer overnight. The next morning, most of the neophytes declined the offer. They said that they were poor and would be better off at the mission.

▲
Juan Bautista Alvarado talking to the neophytes

Another official, Juan Bautista Alvarado, thought that the neophytes didn't understand the benefits of secularization, so he jumped on a *carreta*, or cart, to address the crowd. After he discussed emancipation, he told those who wanted to leave to stand to the right. Anyone wishing to stay was to stand to the left. Most of the neophytes went to the left, showing that they wanted to stay. The Salinan said, "We want to

▲
Many Indians became vaqueros, *working on the California* ranchos.

remain with the padre [the friar]. He is very good to us and we like him."

On August 9, 1834, the Mexican government seized the mission. The friars were allowed to stay and conduct church activities, but they could no longer make the neophytes work or tell them what to do. The government appointed Mexican officials to run the mission. The first official was Ignácio Coronél, who arrived on July 14, 1836. Coronél didn't stay long and was replaced by Ynocente García. Both men were harsh with the Salinan, so many left the mission. Some found jobs as cowboys, called *vaqueros*, or as servants on ranches in the area. Others tried to return to their old villages, but ranchers and settlers had taken their lands, and the old villages no longer existed. Many Salinan had grown up at the mission and didn't know how to live off the land as their ancestors had.

Hunger

As more and more neophytes left the mission, fewer crops were produced. Food became scarce, and starvation gripped Mission San Miguel Arcángel in the late 1830s and early 1840s. Fray Ramón Abella came to Mission San Miguel Arcángel in December 1840.

The mission faced severe food shortages, and Fray Abella had to leave in 1841. He went to Mission San Luis Obispo de Tolosa, where, even though he was close to starvation, he shared his food with the hungry neophytes.

The Mission Is Sold

Under secularization, many mission lands that were supposed to be returned to the California Indians were sold or given away by Mexican officials. Two businessmen, Petronillo Ríos and William Reed, bought

▲
Americans moved to Alta California to find gold.

Mission San Miguel Arcángel in 1846. By this time, Americans were living in the California area. War broke out between the United States and Mexico. The Americans won the war and took possession of Alta California. Soon gold was discovered in Alta California. Many people rushed to the area, hoping to strike it rich. The area became the 31st state in 1850, and its name was shortened to California.

The Americans who took over California also treated the Salinan and other Indians poorly. Like the Spanish, they viewed the Indians as being inferior to themselves. Many of the new American settlers forced the Salinan off their lands. Today, few people of Salinan descent remain. Most of the Salinan either died or joined the American people and the American culture.

The Mission Today

The Mission Is Returned to the Church

Mission San Miguel Arcángel continued to decay. In 1859, the complex was returned to the Catholics by United States president James Buchanan. However, it wasn't until 1878 that Reverend Philip Farrelly was sent to start up a parish church once again. In the meantime, some of the mission buildings were rented out. They were used to house a saloon, a sewing machine store, a dance hall, and living quarters.

President Buchanan

The town of San Miguel began to thrive after 1886, when railroad tracks were laid down near the town, connecting it to Paso Robles and other towns in California. Many Chinese laborers helped build the railroad tracks. Now people could travel easily to and from San Miguel, which increased business in the area. In 1897, the town celebrated its early history by hosting a centennial of the mission's founding. Parades, dancing, lectures, and concerts were included in the celebration.

Many people wanted to restore Mission San Miguel Arcángel, which was crumbling out of neglect. In 1928, the mission was returned to the care of the Franciscan order. The friars began major repairs. Today, Franciscans live at the restored mission, which also serves as a parish church, retreat center, and museum. The mission hosts a *fiesta* on the third Sunday of September each year. At the *fiesta*, visitors can learn more about the mission's history.

Friars still live and work at Mission San Miguel Arcángel. This man, standing next to the statue of Fray Serra, is studying to become a Franciscan friar.

49

Neophytes cooked in ovens like this one at Mission San Miguel Arcángel.

Many students visit the mission's museum to see how the friars and Salinan Indians lived years ago. Visitors can walk through an old kitchen and see a brick oven that the neophytes used for baking. They can visit the friars' living quarters, view their rustic beds and other furniture, and see windows that are still covered with sheepskin. Tools, a loom, a wine vat, and pigments like those used by the Salinan are also on display. Baskets made by California Indians, artifacts from the railroad's Chinese workers, and vestments worn by the friars are included in the museum. Evidence of earthquakes is still visible in the church. Cracks in the plaster run along the walls from the roof to the floor. Although the church's artwork has survived remarkably well, some of it shows signs of water stains and cracks.

The influence of the Spanish missions is still evident in California today. Farming and ranching, two skills brought to the area by the Spanish more than 200 years ago, thrive

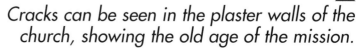

Cracks can be seen in the plaster walls of the church, showing the old age of the mission.

in California. The state is now a world leader in agricultural production.

Artifacts and literature about the Salinan people are displayed in the Salinan Nation Adobe Cultural Center. Each year Salinan descendants gather at Mission San Antonio de Padua in Jolon, California, to celebrate their heritage.

Today, Mission San

Artifacts are on display inside the mission.

Miguel Arcángel stands as a monument to the early Californians. It helps

visitors understand what life was like during the late 1700s and early 1800s. The mission complex teaches present-day Americans about the lives of the Salinan and the Catholic friars who helped to make California the success it is today.

The mission today looks much like it did 200 years ago.

51

Make Your Own Model
Mission San Miguel Arcángel

To make your own model of the San Miguel Arcángel mission, you will need:

pencil	foamcore
scissors	corrugated cardboard
ruler	brown paint
Styrofoam	colored paper
X-Acto knife (ask an adult for help)	miniature bell
glue	moss

Directions

Step 1: To make the front and back of the church, cut out two pieces of Styrofoam that are 12" x 9" (30.5 x 22.9 cm).

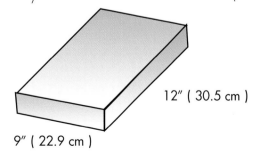
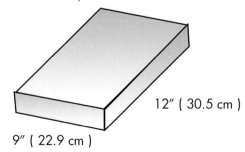

12" (30.5 cm)

9" (22.9 cm)

12" (30.5 cm)

9" (22.9 cm)

Adult supervision is suggested.

Step 2: Choose one of the pieces to be the front and cut out a door with an X-Acto knife.

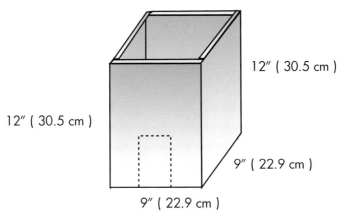

Step 3: Cut two pieces of Styrofoam that are 12″ by 9″ (30.5 x 22.9 cm). These will be the sides of the church.

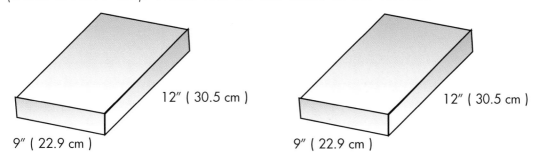

12″ (30.5 cm)

12″ (30.5 cm)

9″ (22.9 cm)

9″ (22.9 cm)

Step 4: Arrange all four pieces in a box shape and glue together. Hold in place for 30 seconds or until the glue dries.

12″ (30.5 cm)

12″ (30.5 cm)

9″ (22.9 cm)

9″ (22.9 cm)

Step 5: Use the large piece of foamcore for the base. Attach the church building to the base with glue.

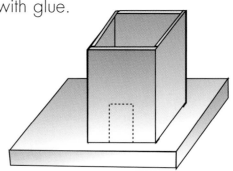

Step 6: Cut out two Styrofoam triangles whose bases are 9" (22.9 cm) long and whose sides are each 6" (15.2 cm). These triangles will be 4" (10.2 cm) high. Glue to the top of the front and back church walls.

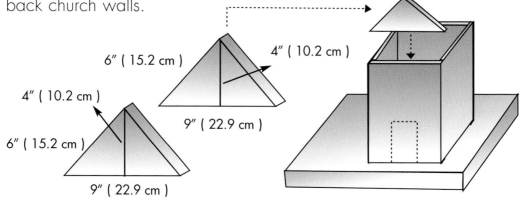

6" (15.2 cm)

4" (10.2 cm)

4" (10.2 cm)

6" (15.2 cm)

9" (22.9 cm)

9" (22.9 cm)

Step 7: To make the arcade, cut two pieces of Styrofoam that are 3" x 7" (7.6 x 17.8 cm). These are the front and back pieces.

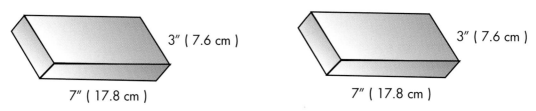

3" (7.6 cm)

3" (7.6 cm)

7" (17.8 cm)

7" (17.8 cm)

Step 8: Trace two arched doorways in the middle of each Styrofoam arcade wall and cut them out with an X-Acto knife.

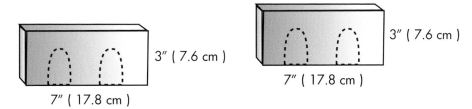

3" (7.6 cm)

7" (17.8 cm)

3" (7.6 cm)

7" (17.8 cm)

Step 9: To make the arcade roof, cut out a piece of cardboard that is 5" by 8" (12.7 x 20.3 cm). Paint the cardboard roof brown. Let paint dry.

5" (12.7 cm)

8" (20.3 cm)

Step 10: Glue the two arcade pieces to the back left side of the church. Then glue the roof to the arcade.

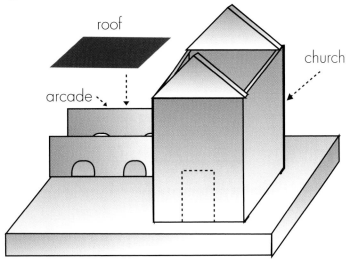

roof

church

arcade

55

Step 11: To make windows on the church, cut out small squares of cardboard and glue them on the building.

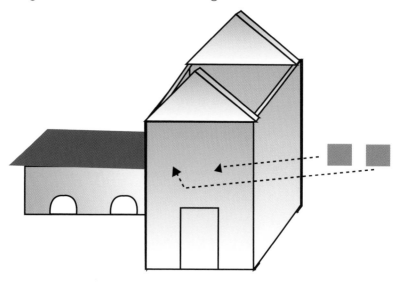

Step 12: Time to decorate! Cut out colored paper in tiny squares and glue them to the floor of the church. Use a round piece of blue paper for an indoor fountain.

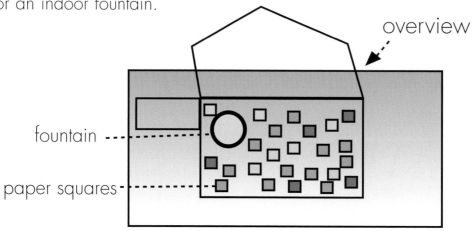

overview

fountain

paper squares

Step 13: Glue a miniature bell in the doorway of the church. Cut paper to make a cross and glue it on the front of the church.

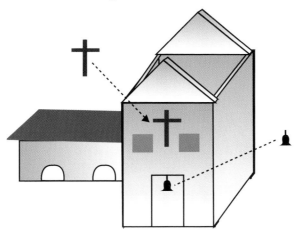

Step 14: Place glue around your mission and arrange moss, dried flowers, or fake plants.

*Use the above mission as a reference for building your mission.

Important Dates in Mission History

1492	Christopher Columbus reaches the West Indies
1542	Cabrillo's expedition to California
1602	Sebastián Vizcaíno sails to California
1713	Fray Junípero Serra is born
1769	Founding of San Diego de Alcalá
1770	Founding of San Carlos Borromeo de Carmelo
1771	Founding of San Antonio de Padua and San Gabriel Arcángel
1772	Founding of San Luis Obispo de Tolosa
1775–76	Founding of San Juan Capistrano
1776	Founding of San Francisco de Asís
1776	Declaration of Independence is signed
1777	Founding of Santa Clara de Asís
1782	Founding of San Buenaventura
1784	Fray Serra dies
1786	Founding of Santa Bárbara
1787	Founding of La Purísima Concepción
1791	Founding of Santa Cruz and Nuestra Señora de la Soledad
1797	**Founding of** San José, San Juan Bautista, **San Miguel Arcángel**, and San Fernando Rey de España
1798	Founding of San Luis Rey de Francia
1804	Founding of Santa Inés
1817	Founding of San Rafael Arcángel
1823	Founding of San Francisco Solano
1849	Gold found in northern California
1850	California becomes the 31st state

Glossary

adobe (uh-DOH-bee) Sun-dried bricks made of straw, mud, and sometimes manure.

baptism (BAP-tih-zum) A ceremony performed when someone is accepted into, or accepts, the Christian faith.

Catholicism (kuh-THAH-lih-sih-zum) The faith or practice of Catholic Christianity, which includes following the spiritual leadership of priests headed by the pope.

Christianity (kris-chee-AH-nih-tee) A religion based on the teachings of Jesus Christ and the Bible, practiced by Eastern, Roman Catholic, and Protestant groups.

complex (KAHM-pleks) A large group of buildings.

convert (kun-VIRT) To change from belief in one religion to belief in another religion.

decree (dih-KREE) An official law or order.

emancipation (ih-man-sih-PAY-shun) Freedom.

Franciscan (fran-SIS-kin) A communal Roman Catholic order of friars, or "brothers," who follow the teachings and example of Saint Francis of Assisi, who did much work as a missionary.

fresco (FRES-koh) A painting made on wet plaster, which lasts longer than a painting made on a dry wall.

friar (FRY-ur) A brother in a communal religious order. Friars can also be priests.

granary (GRAY-nuh-ree) A building where grain is stored.

livestock (LYV-stahk) Farm animals kept for use or profit.

Mass (MAS) A Christian religious ceremony.

neophyte (NEE-oh-fyt) The name for an American Indian once he or she was baptized into the Christian religion.

quarters (KWOR-turz) Rooms where someone lives.

ranching (RAN-ching) Raising cattle, horses, or sheep on a farm.

restoration (res-tuh-RAY-shun) Working to return something, like a building, to its original state.

sanctuary (SAYNK-choo-weh-ree) The sacred part of a church, which contains the altar.

secularization (seh-kyuh-luh-rih-ZAY-shun) Turning over the operation of the mission lands to the Christian Indians.

thatch (THACH) A covering for a house made up of reeds and grass bundled together.

vestments (VEST-mints) Robes that are worn for special ceremonies.

viceroy (VYS-roy) A governor who rules and acts as the representative of the king.

Pronunciation Guide

alcaldes (ahl-KAHL-des)

atole (ah-TOH-lay)

carretas (kah-RAY-tas)

convento (kom-BEN-toh)

fiestas (fee-EHS-tahs)

fray (FRAY)

monjerío (mohn-hay-REE-oh)

pozole (poh-SOH-lay)

ranchería (rahn-cheh-REE-ah)

ranchos (RAHN-chohs)

siesta (see-EHS-tah)

vaqueros (bah-KEH-rohs)

Resources

For more information on the California missions, check out these books and Web sites:

Books:
Lee, Gregory. *California Missions: A Guide to the State's Spanish Heritage.* New York: Renaissance House, 1992.

Tupa, Jerome. *An Uncommon Mission.* San Francisco: Renaissance House, 1992.

Web Sites:
Due to the changing nature of Internet links, PowerKids Press has developed an online list of Web sites related to the subject of this book. This site is updated regularly. Please use this link to access the list: www.powerkidslinks.com/moca/smarc/

Index